Hope

Discover the Life-Changing Power of Hope: A Comprehensive Guide to Overcoming Adversity, Cultivating Resilience, and Achieving Your Wildest Dreams in the Face of Life's Greatest Challenges - The Ultimate Self-Help Resource for Embracing the Power of Positive Thinking and Unleashing Your Full Potential!

Lance P. Richards

Hope: Discover the Life-Changing Power of Hope: A Comprehensive Guide to Overcoming Adversity, Cultivating Resilience, and Achieving Your Wildest Dreams in the Face of Life's Greatest Challenges - The Ultimate Self-Help Resource for Embracing the Power of Positive Thinking and Unleashing Your Full Potential!

Table of Contents

01: The Power of Hope: Understanding the Basics

Hope is a powerful force that has the potential to transform our lives in significant ways. It is the belief that the future can be better than the present and that we have the ability to make positive changes in our lives. Hope provides us with the courage to face life's challenges, to persevere through difficult times, and to see the possibilities that lie ahead. In this chapter, we will explore the basics of hope, including its definition, characteristics, and benefits.

Defining Hope

Hope can be defined as a positive expectation that things will improve or change for the better in the future. It is not a passive waiting for good things to happen but an active process of taking steps to make positive changes in our lives. Hope is not the same as optimism, which is the expectation that things will turn out well regardless of any action on our part. Hope requires action, effort, and a belief that our actions can make a difference in our lives.

Characteristics of Hope

01: THE POWER OF HOPE: UNDERSTANDING THE BASICS

There are several characteristics of hope that distinguish it from other emotional states. These characteristics include:

– Belief in the Possibility of Change - Hope requires a belief that the future can be different from the present and that positive change is possible.

– Motivation to Act - Hope provides the motivation to take action towards positive change.

– Resilience - Hope helps us to bounce back from setbacks and challenges, providing us with the strength to keep moving forward.

– Positive Thinking - Hope is associated with positive thinking, which helps to create a sense of optimism and confidence in our ability to achieve our goals.

– Emotional Well-Being - Hope is associated with better emotional well-being, including reduced anxiety and depression, and greater happiness and life satisfaction.

Benefits of Hope

The benefits of hope are many and significant. Studies have

shown that hope is associated with better health, higher academic achievement, greater job satisfaction, and increased resilience. Hope also provides us with a sense of purpose and meaning in life, which can be especially important during difficult times. Hope helps us to see the possibilities that exist in our lives and to believe that we have the ability to create a better future for ourselves.

Cultivating Hope

Cultivating hope requires effort and intentionality. It involves setting goals, taking action towards those goals, and surrounding ourselves with positive influences. Some ways to cultivate hope include:

– Setting Realistic Goals - Setting goals that are achievable and aligned with our values and passions is key to building hope.

– Taking Action - Taking action towards our goals, even small steps, helps to build momentum and create a sense of progress.

– Surrounding Ourselves with Positive Influences - Sur-

rounding ourselves with positive people, inspirational stor-
ies, and affirming messages can help to build our sense of
hope.

– Practicing Gratitude - Gratitude helps us to focus on the
positive aspects of our lives, creating a sense of optimism
and hope.

Conclusion

Hope is a powerful force that can help us to overcome adversity, build resilience, and achieve our wildest dreams.
Understanding the basics of hope, including its definition,
characteristics, and benefits, is the first step in cultivating
hope in our lives. By setting realistic goals, taking action,
surrounding ourselves with positive influences, and practicing gratitude, we can build our sense of hope and create a
better future for ourselves.

02: How to Identify Hopelessness and Overcome It

While hope is a powerful force that can drive us to achieve our goals and overcome adversity, hopelessness is equally powerful in holding us back and making us feel stuck. Hopelessness is the feeling that things will never change or improve, that we are trapped in our current situation, and that there is no point in trying to make positive changes in our lives. In this chapter, we will explore how to identify hopelessness and overcome it.

Identifying Hopelessness

Hopelessness can manifest in several ways, and it's essential to recognize the signs of hopelessness so we can take action to overcome it. Some common signs of hopelessness include:

– Feeling Stuck - Feeling like we are stuck in our current situation and that nothing will change or improve.

– Negative Thinking - Engaging in negative self-talk, such as telling ourselves that we are not good enough or that we will never succeed.

— Lack of Motivation - Feeling unmotivated to take action towards our goals or to make positive changes in our lives.

— Isolation - Withdrawing from social activities or relationships and feeling a sense of disconnection from others.

— Feelings of Despair - Feeling overwhelmed by life's challenges and that there is no way to overcome them.

Overcoming Hopelessness

While hopelessness can feel all-consuming, there are several steps we can take to overcome it and cultivate hope in our lives. Some ways to overcome hopelessness include:

— Identify the Source - Identifying the root cause of our hopelessness is the first step in overcoming it. We may need to explore our thoughts, feelings, and behaviors to determine what is holding us back.

— Reframe Our Thinking - Reframing our negative thoughts into positive ones can help us shift our mindset from hopelessness to hope. We can challenge our negative self-talk and replace it with affirming messages that promote hope and positivity.

02: HOW TO IDENTIFY HOPELESSNESS AND OVER-COME IT

– Take Action - Taking action towards our goals, no matter how small, can help us build momentum and create a sense of progress. Even small steps can make a significant difference in overcoming hopelessness and building hope.

– Connect with Others - Connecting with others who share our values and passions can help us feel less isolated and provide us with a sense of belonging. We can join groups or communities that align with our interests and goals, or we can seek out supportive relationships with family and friends.

– Seek Help - Seeking help from a mental health professional or support group can be beneficial in overcoming hopelessness. A trained therapist can help us identify the root cause of our hopelessness and provide us with the tools and resources to cultivate hope in our lives.

Conclusion

Hopelessness can feel overwhelming and all-consuming, but with the right tools and resources, we can overcome it and cultivate hope in our lives. By identifying the signs of hopelessness, reframing our thinking, taking action, connecting with others, and seeking help when needed, we can build our sense of hope and create a better future for ourselves. Remember, hope is a powerful force that can transform our lives, and we all have the ability to cultivate it within ourselves.

03: Harnessing the Power of Positive Thinking

Positive thinking is a powerful tool that can transform our mindset, boost our confidence, and help us overcome challenges. The way we think and talk to ourselves can greatly impact our outlook on life, and positive thinking can help us cultivate hope, resilience, and a sense of purpose. In this chapter, we will explore the benefits of positive thinking and provide practical strategies for harnessing its power.

Benefits of Positive Thinking

Positive thinking has several benefits that can improve our overall well-being and quality of life. Some of these benefits include:

– Improved Mental Health - Positive thinking can improve our mood, reduce stress and anxiety, and increase our sense of happiness and well-being.

– Increased Resilience - Positive thinking can help us bounce back from setbacks and challenges and maintain a sense of hope and optimism, even in difficult times.

– Better Physical Health - Positive thinking can improve

03: HARNESSING THE POWER OF POSITIVE THINKING

our physical health by reducing stress, lowering blood pressure, and strengthening our immune system.

– Increased Motivation - Positive thinking can increase our motivation to pursue our goals and make positive changes in our lives.

Strategies for Harnessing the Power of Positive Thinking

While positive thinking may not come naturally to everyone, there are several strategies we can use to cultivate this mindset and harness its power. Some of these strategies include:

– Reframing Negative Thoughts - We can reframe negative thoughts into positive ones by challenging the negative self-talk that holds us back and replacing it with affirming messages. For example, if we think, "I can't do this," we can reframe that thought into "I can do this with practice and effort."

– Gratitude Practice - Practicing gratitude by focusing on what we are thankful for can help us cultivate a positive mindset and increase our sense of happiness and well-being. We can keep a gratitude journal or take time each day to reflect on what we are grateful for.

– Visualization - Visualizing ourselves succeeding and achieving our goals can help us build confidence and maintain a sense of hope and optimism. We can visualize ourselves taking steps towards our goals and see ourselves succeeding.

– Positive Affirmations - Repeating positive affirmations to ourselves can help us cultivate a positive mindset and increase our confidence. We can choose affirmations that align with our goals and values and repeat them to ourselves regularly.

– Surrounding Ourselves with Positive People - Surrounding ourselves with positive, supportive people can help us maintain a positive mindset and increase our motivation to pursue our goals. We can seek out relationships with people who share our values and support our dreams.

Conclusion

Positive thinking is a powerful tool that can help us cultivate hope, resilience, and a sense of purpose. By reframing negative thoughts, practicing gratitude, visualizing success, using positive affirmations, and surrounding ourselves with positive people, we can harness the power of positive thinking and transform our mindset. Remember, the way we think and talk to ourselves can greatly impact our outlook on life, and by choosing to focus on the positive, we can create a better future for ourselves.

04: Mindfulness and Hope: Living in the Present Moment

In today's fast-paced world, it can be easy to get caught up in worries about the future or regrets about the past. Mindfulness is a powerful tool that can help us cultivate a sense of peace, awareness, and hope by living in the present moment. In this chapter, we will explore the benefits of mindfulness, provide practical strategies for living in the present moment, and discuss how mindfulness can help us cultivate hope.

Benefits of Mindfulness

Mindfulness is the practice of being fully present in the moment, without judgment or distraction. The benefits of mindfulness include:

– Reduced Stress and Anxiety - Mindfulness can reduce stress and anxiety by helping us focus on the present moment and letting go of worries about the future or regrets about the past.

– Increased Self-Awareness - Mindfulness can increase our self-awareness by helping us notice our thoughts, emotions, and physical sensations without judgment or attachment.

– Improved Relationships - Mindfulness can improve our relationships by helping us become more present and attentive in our interactions with others.

– Increased Focus and Productivity - Mindfulness can improve our focus and productivity by helping us stay present and engaged in our work.

Strategies for Living in the Present Moment

Living in the present moment is not always easy, but there are several strategies we can use to cultivate mindfulness and stay present. Some of these strategies include:

– Mindful Breathing - Taking deep, intentional breaths and focusing on the sensations of the breath can help us stay present and calm in the moment.

– Body Scan - A body scan involves focusing on the sensations in different parts of the body, from the toes to the head. This can help us become more aware of our physical sensations and stay present.

04: MINDFULNESS AND HOPE: LIVING IN THE PRESENT MOMENT

– Mindful Eating - Paying attention to the flavors, textures, and smells of our food can help us stay present and savor the moment.

– Mindful Walking - Focusing on the sensations of our feet touching the ground and the movement of our body can help us stay present during a walk or exercise.

– Mindful Listening - When listening to others, we can focus on their words, tone, and body language, and avoid getting distracted by our own thoughts or judgments.

Mindfulness and Hope

Mindfulness can help us cultivate a sense of hope by allowing us to fully experience the present moment without the distractions of the past or future. When we are mindful, we can notice the beauty and joy in our lives, even during difficult times. We can also observe our thoughts and emotions without judgment or attachment, which can help us cultivate a sense of hope and perspective. By focusing on the present moment and being aware of our thoughts and emotions, we can identify patterns of negative thinking or hopelessness and work to reframe them into positive, hopeful thoughts.

Conclusion

Mindfulness is a powerful tool that can help us cultivate a sense of peace, awareness, and hope by living in the present moment. By practicing mindful breathing, body scans, eating, walking, and listening, we can stay present and engaged in our lives. Mindfulness can also help us cultivate a sense of hope by allowing us to observe our thoughts and emotions without judgment or attachment, and identify patterns of negative thinking that may be holding us back. Remember, the present moment is where life is happening, and by staying mindful and present, we can cultivate a deeper sense of hope and purpose in our lives.

05: Gratitude and Hope: Cultivating an Attitude of Gratefulness

Introduction:

Gratitude is one of the most important virtues that can transform our lives. It is a powerful tool that can help us to see the good in everything and appreciate the blessings we have. When we cultivate an attitude of gratitude, we become more optimistic, happy, and hopeful. This chapter will explore the benefits of gratitude and provide practical tips on how to cultivate this powerful attitude.

Benefits of Gratitude:

Gratitude has numerous benefits for our mental and emotional health. It helps us to focus on the positive aspects of our lives and appreciate the good things we have. Some of the benefits of gratitude include:

– Improved mental health: Gratitude has been shown to reduce symptoms of depression and anxiety. When we focus on the positive aspects of our lives, we are less likely to dwell on negative thoughts and feelings.

– Increased resilience: When we face challenges and difficulties, gratitude can help us to stay positive and hopeful. It helps us to find the silver lining in difficult situations and see the opportunities for growth.

– Better relationships: Gratitude can improve our relationships with others. When we express gratitude to others, it strengthens our connections and creates a positive atmosphere.

– Better physical health: Gratitude has been linked to better physical health, including improved sleep, reduced stress, and lower blood pressure.

Cultivating an Attitude of Gratitude:

Now that we understand the benefits of gratitude, let's explore some practical tips on how to cultivate this attitude.

– Keep a gratitude journal: A gratitude journal is a powerful tool that can help us to focus on the positive aspects of our lives. Each day, write down three things you are grateful for. This practice will help you to see the good in everything and develop a more positive outlook on life.

– Express gratitude to others: When we express gratitude to

others, it not only benefits them but also ourselves. Take the time to thank the people in your life who have made a difference, whether it's a friend, family member, or colleague.

– Practice mindfulness: Mindfulness is the practice of being present in the moment and fully engaged in what we are doing. When we practice mindfulness, we are more likely to notice the good things in our lives and appreciate them.

– Focus on abundance: Instead of focusing on what we don't have, we should focus on what we do have. When we appreciate the abundance in our lives, we become more grateful for the blessings we have.

– Make gratitude a daily practice: Gratitude is not just a one-time activity but a daily practice. Make it a habit to focus on the positive aspects of your life and express gratitude to others.

Conclusion:

Gratitude is a powerful tool that can transform our lives. When we cultivate an attitude of gratitude, we become more optimistic, happy, and hopeful. This chapter has explored the benefits of gratitude and provided practical tips on how to cultivate this powerful attitude. By practicing gratitude, we can overcome adversity, cultivate resilience, and achieve our wildest dreams.

06: How to Build Resilience and Bounce Back from Adversity

Life is full of ups and downs, and inevitably, we all face adversity at some point. Whether it's losing a job, experiencing a breakup, or dealing with a health crisis, adversity can be difficult to navigate. But the good news is that building resilience can help us bounce back from even the toughest of situations. Resilience is the ability to adapt and cope with stress, adversity, and trauma, and it's a skill that can be developed and strengthened.

In this chapter, we'll explore the different ways you can build resilience and cultivate the ability to bounce back from adversity.

– Develop a positive mindset: A positive mindset is key to building resilience. Instead of focusing on what went wrong, try to reframe the situation and focus on what you can do to move forward. Believe that you have the power to overcome challenges and trust in your ability to do so.

– Practice self-care: Taking care of yourself physically and emotionally is crucial for building resilience. Make sure you're getting enough sleep, eating a healthy diet, and engaging in regular exercise. Take time to engage in activities that bring you joy and help you relax, such as reading a book or taking a bath.

– Cultivate social support: Having a strong support system can be incredibly helpful in building resilience. Make sure you have people in your life who you can turn to when you need help or support. This can be friends, family members, or even a therapist.

– Develop problem-solving skills: Being able to problem-solve is an important aspect of building resilience. When faced with a challenge, try to break it down into smaller parts and come up with a plan for how you'll tackle each part. This can help you feel more in control and less over-whelmed.

– Embrace change: Change is a natural part of life, and it can be difficult to navigate. But by embracing change and being open to new experiences, you can build resilience and adapt to new situations more easily.

– Practice mindfulness: Mindfulness can help you stay present and focused on the present moment, rather than worrying about the past or future. By practicing mindfulness, you can reduce stress and anxiety and build resilience.

– Take action: When faced with a challenge, it can be tempting to give up or feel helpless. But taking action, even small steps, can help you feel more in control and build resilience. Identify what you can do to improve the situation and take action.

– Seek professional help: If you're struggling to build resilience or dealing with a particularly difficult challenge, it may be helpful to seek professional help. A therapist or counselor can help you develop coping strategies and build resilience.

By incorporating these strategies into your life, you can build resilience and develop the ability to bounce back from adversity. Remember, resilience is a skill that can be developed and strengthened over time. With practice and persistence, you can cultivate the resilience you need to face life's challenges head-on.

07: Self-Compassion and Hope: Overcoming Self-Doubt and Negative Self-Talk

Self-compassion is a critical aspect of hope, especially when it comes to overcoming self-doubt and negative self-talk. When you are hard on yourself, constantly criticizing and doubting your abilities, it can be challenging to see a bright future, let alone believe that anything is possible.

Self-compassion is the act of treating yourself with the same kindness, concern, and support that you would offer to a good friend. When you practice self-compassion, you become more aware of your inner critic and learn how to challenge it. You learn to be patient and forgiving with yourself and become better equipped to navigate through difficult times.

If you struggle with self-doubt and negative self-talk, it's essential to work on building your self-compassion. Here are some practical tips to get you started:

– Practice mindfulness: Mindfulness can help you become more aware of your thoughts and feelings without judging them. When you can observe your negative self-talk without getting caught up in it, you're less likely to believe it.

– Challenge your inner critic: When you hear your inner critic telling you that you're not good enough or that you'll never succeed, challenge it. Ask yourself if there's any evidence to support what it's saying. If not, tell your inner critic that you don't believe it.

– Practice self-forgiveness: Everyone makes mistakes, and it's essential to learn how to forgive yourself when you do. Remember that you're only human and that making mistakes is a natural part of the learning process.

– Be kind to yourself: Treat yourself with the same kindness and compassion that you would offer to a good friend. Take care of your physical and emotional needs and give yourself time to rest and recharge.

– Practice gratitude: Practicing gratitude can help you focus on the positive aspects of your life. Take time each day to reflect on the things you're grateful for, no matter how small they may seem.

– Seek support: Don't be afraid to reach out to friends, family, or a mental health professional for support. Talking to someone who understands can help you feel less alone and give you the strength to overcome self-doubt and negative self-talk.

Remember, building self-compassion takes time and practice, but it's a critical step towards cultivating hope. When you learn to be kinder to yourself, you become better equipped to navigate through life's challenges and pursue your dreams.

08: The Role of Faith and Spirituality in Hope

Hope is a complex and multifaceted concept that touches on various aspects of our lives, including our beliefs, values, and relationships. For many people, faith and spirituality play an important role in cultivating hope and finding meaning in life's challenges. In this chapter, we will explore the ways in which faith and spirituality can support and enhance hope, as well as how they can sometimes hinder it.

Faith and spirituality can provide a sense of purpose and meaning in life, which is essential for cultivating hope. When we have a strong belief in something greater than ourselves, we can find the strength and resilience to face the difficulties and uncertainties of life. Faith can offer a sense of security and comfort, knowing that we are not alone in our struggles and that there is a higher power guiding us through them.

Many religious and spiritual traditions offer practices that can help us cultivate hope and resilience. Prayer, meditation, and other forms of contemplative practice can help us connect with our inner resources and find a sense of peace and calm in the face of challenges. Community and fellowship with like-minded individuals can also provide a sense of support and encouragement, reminding us that we are not alone in our struggles.

At the same time, it is important to recognize that faith and spirituality can sometimes be a source of conflict and anxiety, especially if our beliefs are rigid and inflexible. When our faith becomes dogmatic and rigid, it can lead to a sense of hopelessness and despair if we experience a crisis of faith or if we feel that our beliefs are being challenged.

Furthermore, faith and spirituality can sometimes be used as a way to avoid dealing with the realities of life. For example, some people may use religion as a way to escape from their problems, instead of confronting them directly. This can lead to a sense of denial and avoidance, which can ultimately undermine our sense of hope and resilience.

Therefore, it is important to approach faith and spirituality with an open and flexible mindset, recognizing that our beliefs may change over time and that there may be multiple paths to finding meaning and purpose in life. By embracing a spirit of curiosity and exploration, we can deepen our understanding of our beliefs and values, and find new ways to connect with our sense of hope and resilience.

In conclusion, faith and spirituality can play a powerful role in cultivating hope and resilience, offering a sense of purpose, meaning, and connection that can help us navigate life's challenges. At the same time, it is important to approach our beliefs with an open and flexible mindset, recognizing that they may change over time and that there may be multiple paths to finding meaning and purpose in life. By embracing a spirit of curiosity and exploration, we can deepen our understanding of ourselves and the world around us, and find new ways to cultivate hope and resilience.

09: Finding Hope in the Midst of Grief and Loss

Introduction

Grief and loss are inevitable aspects of the human experience, and they can leave us feeling hopeless and overwhelmed. Whether we're dealing with the death of a loved one, the end of a relationship, or a significant life transition, it can be difficult to see a way forward. However, it's essential to remember that hope is still possible, even in the midst of grief and loss. In this chapter, we will explore how to find hope in the face of such challenges.

Understanding Grief and Loss

The first step in finding hope in the midst of grief and loss is to understand what it is we're dealing with. Grief is a natural response to loss, and it can manifest in a variety of ways, including sadness, anger, guilt, and regret. It's essential to acknowledge and process these feelings rather than suppressing them, as they are a necessary part of the healing process.

Acceptance

09: FINDING HOPE IN THE MIDST OF GRIEF AND LOSS

One of the most challenging aspects of grief and loss is accepting that what has happened cannot be changed. It's common to feel like we could have done something differently or that we could have prevented the loss from occurring. However, this kind of thinking can prevent us from moving forward and finding hope. Acceptance doesn't mean forgetting or dismissing what has happened; instead, it means acknowledging the reality of the situation and working to find a way forward.

Self-Care

Taking care of ourselves is critical during times of grief and loss. It's essential to prioritize rest, nutrition, and exercise, as well as engaging in activities that bring us joy and comfort. Taking care of our physical health can also help us to manage our emotions and find hope in the future.

Support Systems

Having a support system during times of grief and loss can make all the difference in our ability to find hope. Friends, family, and support groups can offer comfort, encouragement, and understanding, as well as practical help with tasks like cooking, cleaning, and running errands. It's also essential to seek professional help if we're struggling to cope with our emotions or finding it difficult to function in our daily lives.

Finding Meaning

Finding meaning in our experiences is another way to cultivate hope in the face of grief and loss. This can involve looking for the lessons we can learn from the situation, finding ways to honor the memory of what has been lost, or using our experiences to help others who may be going through similar challenges. When we can find meaning in our experiences, it can help us to see that there is a purpose to our pain and that it's possible to find hope in the future.

Conclusion

Grief and loss are challenging, but it's important to remember that hope is still possible. By understanding what we're dealing with, accepting the reality of the situation, taking care of ourselves, building support systems, and finding meaning, we can cultivate hope and find a way forward. While the pain may never completely go away, we can find hope and learn to live with it, allowing us to move forward and live fulfilling lives.

10: Hope and Mental Health: Managing Anxiety and Depression

Hope is a powerful force that can help you overcome even the toughest challenges in life. In this chapter, we will explore the role that hope plays in managing anxiety and depression, two of the most common mental health issues that people face. We will look at the impact of anxiety and depression on your life, the benefits of hope, and practical strategies for cultivating hope to manage these conditions.

Anxiety and depression are two of the most prevalent mental health disorders in the world. Anxiety is a condition characterized by excessive worry and fear that can interfere with your ability to function in your daily life. Depression, on the other hand, is a mood disorder that causes persistent feelings of sadness, hopelessness, and loss of interest in activities that you used to enjoy.

Both anxiety and depression can have a profound impact on your life. They can affect your ability to work, maintain relationships, and participate in social activities. They can also cause physical symptoms such as fatigue, muscle tension, and sleep disturbances.

However, the good news is that hope can be a powerful tool in managing anxiety and depression. Hope can provide a sense of purpose and direction, help you build resilience, and increase your ability to cope with stress and adversity.

Research has shown that people who have a greater sense of hope experience lower levels of anxiety and depression. In fact, hope has been found to be a significant predictor of mental health outcomes in people with a variety of conditions, including cancer, HIV, and chronic pain.

So, how can you cultivate hope to manage anxiety and depression? Here are some practical strategies that you can use:

– Set Realistic Goals

Setting goals that are achievable can help you build hope and motivation. Start small and focus on goals that are within your control. This can be as simple as getting out of bed in the morning, going for a walk, or completing a small task at work. Celebrate each accomplishment and use it as motivation to continue building momentum.

10: HOPE AND MENTAL HEALTH: MANAGING ANXIETY AND DEPRESSION

– Practice Gratitude

Practicing gratitude can help shift your focus away from negative thoughts and emotions. Take time each day to reflect on what you are grateful for, no matter how small it may seem. This could be anything from a supportive friend to a sunny day. Gratitude can help you appreciate the positive aspects of your life and increase your sense of hope.

– Challenge Negative Thoughts

Negative thoughts can be a major obstacle to building hope. When you find yourself having negative thoughts, try to challenge them. Ask yourself if they are based on facts or assumptions. Try to reframe your thoughts in a more positive way. For example, if you are thinking, "I can't do this," reframe it as, "This is challenging, but I can take it one step at a time."

– Engage in Activities That Bring You Joy

Engaging in activities that bring you joy can help you feel more positive and increase your sense of hope. Make time for hobbies or activities that you enjoy, whether it's reading, listening to music, or spending time with friends. This can help you feel more connected and give you a sense of purpose.

– Connect with Others

Connecting with others can be a powerful tool in managing anxiety and depression. Reach out to friends or family members for support, or consider joining a support group. Being around others who are going through similar experiences can help you feel less alone and increase your sense of hope.

– Seek Professional Help

If you are struggling with anxiety or depression, seeking professional help can be an important step in managing your symptoms. A mental health professional can provide you with tools and strategies to manage your condition, and help you build a sense of hope for the future.

In conclusion, hope can be a powerful tool in managing anxiety and depression. By setting realistic goals, practicing gratitude, challenging negative thoughts, engaging in activities that bring you joy, connecting with others, and seeking professional help, you can cultivate hope and build resilience in the face of these challenges.

It's important to remember that managing anxiety and depression is a journey, and there will be ups and downs along the way. But by focusing on the positive, setting achievable goals, and surrounding yourself with a support system, you can build the resilience and hope needed to overcome even the toughest challenges.

In addition to these strategies, there are other lifestyle changes that can be helpful in managing anxiety and depression. For example, getting enough sleep, eating a healthy diet, and getting regular exercise can all have a positive impact on your mental health.

It's also important to remember that seeking professional help is not a sign of weakness. In fact, it takes strength and courage to recognize when you need help and to reach out for it. A mental health professional can provide you with the tools and strategies you need to manage your symptoms and build a sense of hope for the future.

10: HOPE AND MENTAL HEALTH: MANAGING ANXI-
ETY AND DEPRESSION

In summary, hope can be a powerful tool in managing anxiety and depression. By setting achievable goals, practicing gratitude, challenging negative thoughts, engaging in activities that bring you joy, connecting with others, and seeking professional help, you can cultivate hope and build resilience in the face of these challenges. Remember that managing anxiety and depression is a journey, and it's okay to ask for help along the way. With the right tools and support, you can overcome these challenges and achieve your wildest dreams.

11: Building Healthy Relationships: How Hope Can Strengthen Connections

Relationships are a fundamental aspect of the human experience, and they play a crucial role in our overall well-being and happiness. But building and maintaining healthy relationships can be challenging, especially when faced with life's greatest challenges. That's where hope comes in. In this chapter, we'll explore how hope can strengthen connections and build healthy relationships, whether it's with family, friends, or romantic partners.

First and foremost, it's important to understand that hope is not just about positive thinking or wishful thinking. It's a mindset that involves setting realistic goals, believing in yourself, and having the resilience to overcome setbacks and obstacles. When it comes to building healthy relationships, hope can help us to approach others with a sense of optimism, empathy, and understanding.

One way that hope can strengthen connections is by fostering a sense of gratitude and appreciation. When we cultivate hope, we are better able to recognize the good in others and in our relationships. This, in turn, can help us to express gratitude and appreciation for those we care about, which can strengthen the bond between us.

Another way that hope can strengthen relationships is by helping us to navigate conflict and challenges. No relationship is perfect, and conflicts and challenges are inevitable. However, when we approach these difficulties with a sense of hope and optimism, we are better able to communicate effectively, find common ground, and work together to overcome the problem.

Hope can also help us to build deeper connections with others by fostering a sense of empathy and compassion. When we approach others with hope, we are more likely to see things from their perspective and to empathize with their struggles. This, in turn, can help us to build deeper connections and to be more supportive and understanding in our relationships.

Of course, building healthy relationships is not just about cultivating hope within ourselves. It also involves being intentional about our interactions with others. This includes being present and attentive, actively listening, and showing interest and curiosity in others' lives and experiences.

In romantic relationships, hope can be especially important. When we approach our partners with a sense of hope and optimism, we are better able to communicate effectively, express our needs and desires, and build a strong emotional connection. This can lead to greater intimacy, trust, and commitment in the relationship.

However, it's important to remember that building healthy relationships takes work, and it's not always easy. It's normal to experience conflicts, misunderstandings, and setbacks along the way. But by approaching these challenges with a sense of hope and resilience, we can strengthen our connections and build deeper, more meaningful relationships with those we care about.

In summary, hope can be a powerful tool in building healthy relationships. By fostering a sense of gratitude, navigating conflict with optimism, showing empathy and compassion, and being intentional in our interactions, we can build stronger connections with those we care about. Remember that building healthy relationships takes work, but with hope, resilience, and a willingness to learn and grow,

11: BUILDING HEALTHY RELATIONSHIPS: HOW HOPE CAN STRENGTHEN CONNECTIONS

anything is possible.

12: The Power of Forgiveness in Cultivating Hope

Forgiveness is a powerful tool that can help us to let go of negative emotions, heal from past hurts, and cultivate hope for the future. In this chapter, we'll explore the role of forgiveness in cultivating hope, and how we can use this powerful tool to overcome adversity and achieve our goals.

First, it's important to understand what forgiveness is, and what it is not. Forgiveness is not about condoning or excusing the actions of others, nor is it about forgetting or minimizing the harm that was done. Instead, forgiveness is about choosing to let go of anger, resentment, and bitterness, and moving forward with a sense of compassion, empathy, and hope.

When we hold onto anger, resentment, and bitterness towards others, we are allowing those negative emotions to control our lives. These emotions can weigh us down, hold us back, and prevent us from moving forward with a sense of hope and optimism. By choosing to forgive, we are taking back control of our lives and freeing ourselves from the burden of negative emotions.

12: THE POWER OF FORGIVENESS IN CULTIVATING HOPE

Forgiveness can also help us to heal from past hurts and trauma. When we hold onto anger and resentment, we are often replaying the past in our minds, reliving the hurt and pain over and over again. This can prevent us from moving forward and making progress towards our goals. By choosing to forgive, we are breaking free from the past and opening ourselves up to new opportunities for growth and healing.

In addition, forgiveness can help us to build stronger relationships with others. When we choose to forgive, we are demonstrating empathy, compassion, and understanding towards others. This can help to build trust and deepen our connections with others, which can in turn lead to greater opportunities for personal and professional growth.

Of course, forgiveness is not always easy. It can be a challenging and sometimes painful process, especially when the hurt we have experienced is deep and long-lasting. However, it's important to remember that forgiveness is a choice, and it's one that we can make at any time, regardless of how difficult it may seem.

There are many strategies that can be helpful in cultivating forgiveness. One of the most important is to practice self-compassion. When we are able to be kind and understanding towards ourselves, we are better able to extend that same compassion to others. This can make it easier to let go of negative emotions and move forward with a sense of hope and optimism.

Another helpful strategy is to focus on the positive. Instead of dwelling on the hurt and pain that was caused, try to focus on the good in your life and in your relationships. This can help to shift your perspective and make forgiveness feel more achievable.

In summary, forgiveness is a powerful tool that can help us to let go of negative emotions, heal from past hurts, and cultivate hope for the future. By choosing to forgive, we are taking back control of our lives and freeing ourselves from the burden of anger, resentment, and bitterness. While forgiveness is not always easy, it is a choice that we can make at any time, and it has the potential to transform our lives in profound ways.

13: Overcoming Addiction: Hope as a Key Component of Recovery

Addiction is a complex and challenging issue that affects millions of people worldwide. It is a disease that impacts not only the individual struggling with it but also their loved ones and the broader community. However, there is hope for those struggling with addiction. With the right tools and support, it is possible to overcome addiction and achieve long-term recovery.

One of the key components of addiction recovery is hope. When someone is in the grips of addiction, it can be difficult to see a way out or imagine a life without substance use. However, hope can provide a glimmer of light in the darkness, helping individuals to see a future filled with possibilities and potential.

Hope can be a powerful motivator for change. When individuals have hope for the future, they are more likely to take the necessary steps to achieve their goals and overcome their addiction. It can provide the strength and resilience needed to weather the challenges that come with recovery.

Here are some ways in which hope can play a key role in ad-

13: OVERCOMING ADDICTION: HOPE AS A KEY COMPONENT OF RECOVERY

diction recovery:

– Inspiring Change: Hope can inspire individuals to make positive changes in their lives. When they have hope for a brighter future, they are more likely to take action to achieve their goals, including seeking treatment for their addiction.

– Building Resilience: Addiction recovery can be a challenging and sometimes painful process. However, when individuals have hope, they are better able to weather the difficulties and setbacks that may come their way. Hope can help to build resilience and strength, allowing individuals to stay committed to their recovery goals.

– Cultivating Positive Mindset: Hope can help to cultivate a positive mindset that is essential for addiction recovery. By focusing on the possibilities and potential for the future, individuals can shift their focus away from negative thoughts and emotions that may have contributed to their addiction.

– Creating Support Networks: Hope can also help individuals to build supportive relationships with others. When individuals have hope for the future, they are more likely to

reach out to others for help and support. This can be a critical component of addiction recovery, as the support of others can help individuals stay committed to their recovery
goals.

There are many strategies that can help individuals to cultivate hope in addiction recovery. Here are a few:

— Setting Goals: Setting achievable goals can provide a
sense of purpose and direction that can help individuals to
maintain hope for the future.

— Seeking Support: Building a support network of friends,
family, and healthcare professionals can help individuals to
stay motivated and committed to their recovery goals.

— Practicing Gratitude: Focusing on the positive aspects of
life and expressing gratitude for the things we have can help
to cultivate a sense of hope and optimism.

— Celebrating Progress: Celebrating even small wins can
help individuals to maintain a positive outlook and stay motivated to continue their recovery journey.

In summary, hope is a critical component of addiction recovery. It can inspire change, build resilience, cultivate positive mindset, and create supportive relationships. By cultivating hope and committing to recovery, individuals struggling with addiction can overcome their challenges and achieve a fulfilling life in recovery.

14: Hope and Healing: Exploring the Connection

Hope and healing are deeply interconnected. In the face of adversity or illness, hope can provide a sense of optimism and motivation to persevere through the challenges and pursue a path toward healing. Likewise, healing can strengthen one's sense of hope and reinforce the belief in the power of positive thinking.

In this chapter, we will explore the connection between hope and healing and provide practical strategies for cultivating hope in the face of illness, injury, or other forms of adversity.

Hope and Healing: The Connection

Hope is a powerful force that can positively impact the healing process in many ways. Here are some examples:

– Psychological Benefits: Hope can provide psychological benefits, such as reduced stress, anxiety, and depression, which can improve overall well-being and support the body's natural healing processes.

– Positive Outlook: A positive outlook can impact how the

body responds to treatment, as a hopeful and optimistic attitude can help individuals to better cope with the challenges of healing and stay committed to their recovery
goals.

– Motivation: Hope can provide motivation and drive to
continue to pursue healing even in the face of setbacks and
challenges. This can help individuals to stay focused on
their goals and maintain a sense of purpose during the healing process.

– Social Support: Cultivating hope can also help individuals
to build strong social support networks, which can provide
emotional and practical support during the healing process.

Cultivating Hope in the Healing Process

Here are some practical strategies for cultivating hope during the healing process:

– Practice Positive Thinking: Focus on positive thoughts
and affirmations, and surround yourself with people who
uplift and inspire you.

– Set Goals: Setting small, achievable goals can help to

maintain a sense of purpose and progress, even when heal-ing feels slow or stagnant.

– Build Social Support: Connect with friends, family, and healthcare professionals who can provide emotional and practical support during the healing process.

– Mind-Body Practices: Mind-body practices such as medit-ation, yoga, and deep breathing can help to reduce stress and promote relaxation, which can support the body's nat-ural healing processes.

– Gratitude Practice: Practice gratitude by reflecting on the things in your life that you are thankful for. This can help to shift your focus away from negative thoughts and emotions and promote a more positive outlook.

– Self-Care: Take care of your physical, emotional, and mental health by eating a healthy diet, getting enough rest, and engaging in activities that promote relaxation and well-being.

Healing and Hope: A Shared Journey

Healing and hope are both journeys that require time, effort, and dedication. However, they are also journeys that are best taken together. By cultivating hope, individuals can build the resilience and motivation needed to pursue healing, while healing can reinforce one's belief in the power of hope and positive thinking.

In conclusion, hope and healing are deeply interconnected, and cultivating hope can positively impact the healing process in many ways. By practicing positive thinking, setting goals, building social support, engaging in mind-body practices, and practicing self-care, individuals can cultivate hope and pursue a path toward healing and wellness.

15: Hope and Creativity: Using Imagination to Achieve Your Dreams

Introduction

Hope and creativity are closely linked. Hope can inspire creativity, and creativity can fuel hope. When we imagine a better future, we tap into our creative potential and envision ways to make that future a reality. In this chapter, we'll explore the connection between hope and creativity and discuss how you can use your imagination to achieve your dreams.

The Connection Between Hope and Creativity

Hope is often associated with optimism and positive thinking, which can provide the foundation for creative thinking. When we feel hopeful, we're more likely to see possibilities instead of limitations. This mindset can help us find new solutions to problems, generate new ideas, and take risks. Hope can also give us the courage to try new things, fail, and try again until we succeed.

Creativity, in turn, can help us maintain hope. When we're

creative, we're engaging our minds in a positive way, which can help us cope with stress and negative emotions. Creativity can provide an outlet for self-expression, help us build resilience, and improve our mental health.

Using Imagination to Achieve Your Dreams

Imagination is a powerful tool that can help us achieve our dreams. When we use our imaginations, we can visualize the future we want and create a roadmap for getting there. Here are some ways to tap into your imagination and use it to achieve your goals:

— Visualize success: Spend some time imagining yourself achieving your goals. Picture yourself in the future, living the life you want, and feeling fulfilled. This visualization can help you stay motivated and focused on your goals.

— Brainstorm creative solutions: When faced with a challenge, don't limit yourself to traditional solutions. Instead, use your imagination to come up with new and innovative ideas. Write down all your ideas, even the ones that seem impossible, and then evaluate them to see which ones are feasible.

15: HOPE AND CREATIVITY: USING IMAGINATION TO ACHIEVE YOUR DREAMS

– Use creative outlets to process emotions: Creative outlets like writing, painting, or music can help us process our emotions and work through difficult experiences. By expressing ourselves creatively, we can gain new insights, find solutions to problems, and move forward with hope.

– Collaborate with others: Collaboration can be a powerful way to spark creativity and generate new ideas. Work with others who share your vision and values to brainstorm solutions and develop plans for achieving your goals.

– Take risks: Creativity often involves taking risks and trying new things. When you're feeling stuck, try something outside of your comfort zone. You might discover a new passion or talent that can help you achieve your dreams.

Conclusion

Hope and creativity are essential components of achieving our goals and living fulfilling lives. By tapping into our imaginations, we can cultivate hope, generate new ideas, and find innovative solutions to challenges. Whether you're an artist, an entrepreneur, or simply someone looking to improve your life, embracing creativity and hope can help you

15: HOPE AND CREATIVITY: USING IMAGINATION TO ACHIEVE YOUR DREAMS

achieve your wildest dreams.

16: Hope and Self-Discovery: Embracing Your Unique Identity

Introduction

In our quest to discover the power of hope, we often overlook the importance of self-discovery in cultivating hope. Knowing who we are and what we stand for can give us a sense of purpose, clarity, and direction in life. It can also help us identify our strengths and weaknesses, set meaningful goals, and live authentically.

In this chapter, we will explore the relationship between hope and self-discovery, and how embracing your unique identity can fuel your hope and help you achieve your wildest dreams.

Understanding Your Identity

Identity refers to the qualities, beliefs, values, and experiences that define who we are. Our identity is shaped by various factors such as our family background, cultural heritage, social environment, personal experiences, and individual choices.

Self-discovery involves a process of introspection and reflection that helps us uncover our true identity. It requires us to explore our thoughts, emotions, desires, and behaviors in a non-judgmental and compassionate manner. It also involves challenging our assumptions, biases, and limiting beliefs that may prevent us from fully embracing our authentic selves.

The Importance of Self-Discovery in Cultivating Hope

Self-discovery is a crucial component of cultivating hope. When we know who we are and what we stand for, we can develop a sense of purpose and direction in life. We can set meaningful goals that align with our values and beliefs, and pursue them with passion and conviction.

Self-discovery also helps us identify our strengths and weaknesses. We can leverage our strengths to achieve our goals and overcome obstacles, and work on our weaknesses to improve ourselves and become more resilient. By knowing ourselves, we can develop a sense of self-efficacy, which is the belief in our ability to achieve our goals and succeed in life.

Embracing Your Unique Identity

16: HOPE AND SELF-DISCOVERY: EMBRACING YOUR UNIQUE IDENTITY

Embracing your unique identity is an essential aspect of self-discovery. It means accepting yourself for who you are, including your strengths and weaknesses, quirks and imperfections, and past mistakes and failures. It also means acknowledging your values, beliefs, and passions that make you who you are.

When you embrace your unique identity, you can develop a sense of self-worth and self-acceptance. You can recognize that you are a valuable and worthy human being, regardless of your achievements or external circumstances. This can help you cultivate hope and resilience, even in the face of adversity.

Using Your Unique Identity to Achieve Your Dreams

Embracing your unique identity can also help you achieve your wildest dreams. By knowing who you are and what you stand for, you can set meaningful goals that align with your values and passions. You can also leverage your strengths and unique qualities to achieve your goals in a way that feels authentic and fulfilling.

For example, if you are a creative person, you can use your

imagination and innovative thinking to come up with new and exciting ideas for your career or personal life. If you are a compassionate and empathetic person, you can use your skills to help others and make a positive impact in the world.

Conclusion

In conclusion, self-discovery is a crucial component of cultivating hope and achieving your wildest dreams. By understanding your identity, embracing your unique qualities, and leveraging them to pursue your goals, you can develop a sense of purpose, direction, and fulfillment in life. When you know who you are and what you stand for, you can cultivate hope and resilience, even in the face of life's greatest challenges.

17: Cultivating a Support System: The Role of Community in Hope

Introduction:

As human beings, we are social creatures who thrive on connection and community. Having a strong support system is crucial to our well-being and our ability to cultivate hope, especially during times of adversity. In this chapter, we will explore the role of community in fostering hope and provide strategies for building and maintaining a support system.

Why Community Matters:

When we face challenges, we often feel isolated and alone. However, being a part of a supportive community can make all the difference in our ability to cope and overcome adversity. A community can provide a sense of belonging, validation, and emotional support. Additionally, being part of a community can help us feel more empowered, as we are surrounded by people who share similar values and goals.

Building a Support System:

Building a support system takes effort and intentionality. It is important to identify the people in our lives who are supportive and who we can rely on during difficult times. This can include family members, friends, coworkers, and even online communities. Once we have identified our support system, it is important to nurture those relationships by being present, showing gratitude, and offering support when needed.

Finding a Community:

Sometimes, it can be difficult to find a supportive community. However, there are many resources available for connecting with others who share similar experiences and interests. This can include joining clubs or groups based on hobbies or interests, attending events or workshops, or joining online communities.

Supporting Others:

Being part of a community is not just about receiving support, but also about giving it. It is important to be there for others and offer support when needed. This can include listening, offering advice or resources, or simply being present. By supporting others, we can strengthen our own sense of purpose and well-being.

Conclusion:

In conclusion, community plays a vital role in our ability to cultivate hope and overcome adversity. Building and maintaining a support system takes effort and intentionality, but the rewards are immeasurable. By connecting with others who share our values and goals, we can feel a sense of belonging, validation, and empowerment. Additionally, being part of a community allows us to support others and strengthen our own sense of purpose and well-being.

18: Hope and Goal-Setting: Turning Dreams into Reality

Setting and achieving goals is a crucial part of living a hopeful life. When we have hope, we have a sense of purpose and direction. We know where we are going and what we want to achieve. Without hope, we can easily become lost and directionless.

Goals give us something to strive for and help us measure our progress. When we set a goal, we are creating a vision of what we want our future to look like. This vision provides us with motivation and energy to take action towards our desired outcome.

However, setting goals can be challenging, especially when we are facing difficult circumstances. It's important to remember that setting realistic goals is key to achieving them. Unrealistic or unattainable goals can lead to disappointment and feelings of failure.

One way to set realistic goals is to use the SMART goal-setting framework. SMART stands for Specific, Measurable, Achievable, Relevant, and Time-bound. Let's take a closer look at each of these components:

18: HOPE AND GOAL-SETTING: TURNING DREAMS INTO REALITY

– Specific: Your goal should be clearly defined and specific. Instead of setting a vague goal like "lose weight," try setting a specific goal like "lose 10 pounds in three months."

– Measurable: Your goal should be measurable so that you can track your progress. This means setting concrete criteria for what you want to achieve. For example, if your goal is to read more, you might set a goal to read for 30 minutes every day.

– Achievable: Your goal should be achievable, meaning that it is possible for you to accomplish with effort and commitment. Be realistic about what you can achieve given your current circumstances.

– Relevant: Your goal should be relevant to your overall vision for your life. It should be something that is important to you and aligns with your values and priorities.

– Time-bound: Your goal should have a deadline or specific timeline for completion. This helps create a sense of urgency and keeps you motivated to work towards your goal.

Using the SMART framework can help you set goals that are

realistic, achievable, and meaningful. It can also help you break down your larger goals into smaller, more manageable steps. This can be particularly helpful when you are facing a big challenge or feeling overwhelmed.

In addition to setting SMART goals, it's important to cultivate a sense of hope and optimism when working towards your goals. This can help you stay motivated and resilient in the face of setbacks and obstacles. Here are some tips for cultivating hope while pursuing your goals:

— Practice positive self-talk: Monitor your self-talk and try to replace negative thoughts with positive ones. For example, instead of thinking "I'll never be able to do this," try thinking "I can do this if I keep trying."

— Celebrate small successes: Recognize and celebrate the small successes along the way. This can help keep you motivated and focused on your progress.

— Visualize success: Use visualization techniques to imagine yourself successfully achieving your goals. This can help you build confidence and stay motivated.

18: HOPE AND GOAL-SETTING: TURNING DREAMS INTO REALITY

— Stay flexible: Remember that setbacks and obstacles are a normal part of the process. Be open to adjusting your goals or approach as needed.

— Seek support: Lean on your support system for encouragement and guidance. This might include friends, family, or a therapist.

Remember that setting and achieving goals is a process. It takes time, effort, and commitment. But with hope and a clear vision for the future, you can turn your dreams into reality.

19: Overcoming Setbacks and Obstacles: Persevering Through Challenges

Introduction

Setbacks and obstacles are inevitable in life. Whether it's a failure at work, a personal loss, or a health challenge, these difficulties can leave us feeling overwhelmed and helpless. But with hope as our guide, we can overcome these challenges and emerge stronger and more resilient. In this chapter, we will explore the power of hope in overcoming setbacks and obstacles, and the strategies we can use to persevere through challenging times.

The Power of Hope in Overcoming Setbacks and Obstacles

Hope is a vital ingredient in our ability to overcome setbacks and obstacles. When we have hope, we have a sense of purpose and direction, even in the midst of difficult circumstances. We believe that our goals and dreams are achievable, and we are willing to put in the effort to make them a reality. Hope gives us the strength and resilience to keep going, even when we encounter obstacles along the way.

19: OVERCOMING SETBACKS AND OBSTACLES: PERSEVERING THROUGH CHALLENGES

Research has shown that hope can have a positive impact on our mental health and well-being. People with high levels of hope are more likely to experience lower levels of anxiety and depression, and higher levels of happiness and life satisfaction. They are also more resilient in the face of stress and adversity, and are better able to cope with difficult situations.

Strategies for Persevering Through Challenges

While hope is a powerful tool for overcoming setbacks and obstacles, it is not enough on its own. We also need to develop strategies for persevering through challenges. Here are some strategies that can help:

– Embrace a growth mindset

A growth mindset is the belief that our abilities and talents can be developed through hard work, practice, and perseverance. When we have a growth mindset, we see challenges as opportunities for growth and learning, rather than as insurmountable obstacles. We are more likely to persist in the face of setbacks, because we believe that we can improve and get better over time.

19: OVERCOMING SETBACKS AND OBSTACLES: PER-SEVERING THROUGH CHALLENGES

– Practice self-compassion

Self-compassion is the practice of treating ourselves with kindness, understanding, and acceptance, especially in the face of difficulties and setbacks. When we practice self-compassion, we are less likely to be critical and judgmental of ourselves, and more likely to be patient and supportive. This can help us cope with challenging situations more effectively, and prevent us from getting stuck in negative self-talk and rumination.

– Build a support network

Having a strong support network is essential for persevering through challenges. We need people in our lives who can offer us encouragement, support, and practical help when we need it. This can include friends, family members, mentors, or support groups. Building and maintaining these connections can help us stay motivated and focused, even in the face of adversity.

– Take action

When we encounter setbacks and obstacles, it can be easy to

feel overwhelmed and powerless. But taking action, even small steps, can help us regain a sense of control and momentum. This might involve breaking down a large goal into smaller, more manageable tasks, or seeking out resources and support to help us move forward. By taking action, we can build our confidence and resilience, and move closer to our goals.

Conclusion

Setbacks and obstacles are a natural part of life, but with hope and perseverance, we can overcome them and achieve our dreams. By embracing a growth mindset, practicing self-compassion, building a support network, and taking action, we can stay motivated and focused even in the face of adversity. With these strategies in our toolkit, we can cultivate the power of hope and achieve our wildest dreams.

20: The Science of Hope: Understanding the Neurological Basis

The concept of hope has been around for centuries and has been studied by many scholars, philosophers, and scientists. However, it was only in the last few decades that the neuroscience of hope has started to be explored.

The human brain is a complex organ that consists of millions of neurons that are constantly communicating with one another through electrical and chemical signals. It is through this intricate network of neurons that thoughts, emotions, and behaviors are generated. Hope is no exception, and researchers have discovered that there are specific neural pathways that are involved in the experience of hope.

One of the key regions of the brain that is involved in hope is the prefrontal cortex, which is located in the front of the brain. This region is responsible for planning, decision-making, and goal setting, all of which are essential components of hope. When we are hopeful, our prefrontal cortex is activated, and we are better able to imagine positive outcomes and take action to achieve them.

Another important region of the brain that is involved in

hope is the amygdala, which is responsible for processing emotions. The amygdala is activated when we experience fear or anxiety, but it can also be activated when we experience positive emotions, such as hope. When the amygdala is activated, it releases neurotransmitters such as dopamine and serotonin, which are associated with feelings of pleasure and reward.

In addition to these regions of the brain, researchers have also identified several neurotransmitters and hormones that are involved in the experience of hope. For example, serotonin and dopamine are both associated with feelings of pleasure and reward, and are released in response to positive experiences and emotions. Similarly, oxytocin, which is often referred to as the "love hormone," is associated with social bonding and trust, and has been shown to increase feelings of hope and optimism.

The neuroscience of hope has several important implications for our understanding of mental health and well-being. For example, researchers have found that individuals who are more hopeful tend to have better mental health outcomes, including lower levels of anxiety and depression.

20: THE SCIENCE OF HOPE: UNDERSTANDING THE NEUROLOGICAL BASIS

This may be due in part to the fact that hope is associated with increased levels of positive emotions, which can help to counteract the negative emotions that are often associated with mental health problems.

In addition to its role in mental health, hope also plays an important role in physical health. Studies have found that individuals who are more hopeful tend to have better physical health outcomes, including lower levels of inflammation, better immune function, and even longer life spans.

Overall, the neuroscience of hope provides important insights into the mechanisms that underlie this important human experience. By understanding the neural pathways and neurotransmitters that are involved in hope, we can develop more effective interventions for promoting hope and resilience in individuals who are struggling with adversity.

21: Hope and Physical Health: The Mind-Body Connection

Introduction

We often hear the phrase "mind over matter," but did you know that hope can play a vital role in physical health? Hope is not just an abstract concept; it has a tangible impact on our physical well-being. Studies have shown that people who have hope tend to have better physical health outcomes than those who do not. In this chapter, we will explore the link between hope and physical health and discuss some of the ways in which hope can be used as a tool to improve our overall well-being.

The Mind-Body Connection

The mind-body connection refers to the relationship between our mental and physical states. It is the idea that our thoughts, feelings, and emotions can affect our physical health. For example, have you ever felt physically ill when you were stressed or anxious? This is a classic example of the mind-body connection at work.

Research has shown that the mind-body connection can be

a powerful tool for improving physical health outcomes. One way in which this connection can be harnessed is through the use of hope. Hope can help to reduce stress, improve immune function, and even speed up the healing process.

Reducing Stress

Stress is a major contributor to many physical health problems, including heart disease, high blood pressure, and diabetes. One of the ways in which hope can help to improve physical health outcomes is by reducing stress levels. When we feel hopeful, we are less likely to experience the negative effects of stress on our bodies.

Studies have shown that people who have high levels of hope tend to have lower levels of stress. This is because hope helps us to feel more in control of our lives and less anxious about the future. When we feel hopeful, we are more likely to take positive action to improve our situations, which in turn reduces stress levels.

Improving Immune Function

21: HOPE AND PHYSICAL HEALTH: THE MIND-BODY CONNECTION

Another way in which hope can improve physical health outcomes is by boosting immune function. The immune system is responsible for protecting the body against infection and disease. When our immune systems are functioning properly, we are less likely to get sick.

Research has shown that hope can help to improve immune function. When we feel hopeful, our bodies produce more white blood cells, which are an important part of the immune system. This means that people who have high levels of hope are less likely to get sick and more likely to recover quickly when they do.

Speeding Up the Healing Process

Finally, hope can also help to speed up the healing process. When we are recovering from an illness or injury, our bodies need to repair themselves in order to heal. Studies have shown that people who have high levels of hope tend to recover more quickly than those who do not.

This is because hope can help to reduce stress levels and improve immune function, both of which are important factors in the healing process. Additionally, when we feel hopeful, we are more likely to take positive action to support our bodies as they heal, such as getting enough rest and eating a healthy diet.

Conclusion

Hope is a powerful tool for improving physical health outcomes. By reducing stress levels, improving immune function, and speeding up the healing process, hope can help us to live healthier, happier lives. If you are looking to improve your physical health, consider incorporating hope into your daily routine. Whether it's through positive thinking, goal-setting, or cultivating a support system, there are many ways to harness the power of hope to improve your overall well-being.

22: The Power of Visualization: Using Your Imagination to Build Hope

The human imagination is a powerful tool that can be harnessed to create incredible positive change in your life. The art of visualization is the process of creating a mental image or scenario in your mind that helps you to achieve your goals and build hope.

Visualizing your desired outcome is a technique that can be used to help you overcome obstacles and achieve your goals. This technique can be applied to any aspect of your life, from improving your physical health to achieving financial success, and everything in between.

When you visualize your goals, you create a mental picture of what you want to achieve. This mental image can help you to focus on your desired outcome, which in turn can help you to stay motivated and inspired, even in the face of challenges.

Research has shown that visualization can be an effective tool for building hope and increasing resilience. In a study published in the Journal of Behavioral Medicine, researchers found that visualizing positive outcomes can lead to increased feelings of hope, optimism, and self-efficacy.

The power of visualization lies in its ability to help you shift your mindset from one of defeat to one of possibility. By visualizing your desired outcome, you are creating a mental roadmap that can help you to overcome obstacles and achieve your goals.

To get started with visualization, find a quiet place where you can sit or lie down comfortably. Close your eyes and take a few deep breaths. When you feel relaxed and centered, begin to visualize your desired outcome.

For example, if you want to improve your physical health, visualize yourself engaging in physical activity that you enjoy, such as running or swimming. See yourself moving with ease and grace, feeling strong and energized. Imagine yourself reaching your fitness goals, whether that's running a marathon or simply feeling more comfortable in your own skin.

As you visualize your desired outcome, try to engage all of your senses. What do you see, hear, feel, smell, and taste?

22: THE POWER OF VISUALIZATION: USING YOUR IMAGINATION TO BUILD HOPE

The more vividly you can imagine your desired outcome, the more powerful your visualization will be.

It's important to note that visualization alone is not enough to achieve your goals. You still need to take action and put in the work to make your dreams a reality. However, visualization can be a powerful tool to help you stay motivated and focused on your goals, even when the going gets tough.

In addition to visualizing your desired outcome, you can also use visualization to prepare for challenging situations. For example, if you have a difficult conversation coming up with a friend or loved one, you can visualize the conversation going smoothly and calmly. See yourself listening attentively and responding with empathy and understanding. This can help you to feel more confident and prepared when the actual conversation takes place.

Visualization can also be used to build hope and resilience in the face of adversity. If you're going through a difficult time, try visualizing yourself emerging from the situation stronger and more resilient than ever before. See yourself bouncing back from setbacks and finding new opportunities for growth and success.

22: THE POWER OF VISUALIZATION: USING YOUR IMAGINATION TO BUILD HOPE

In conclusion, visualization is a powerful tool for building hope and achieving your goals. By using your imagination to create a mental picture of your desired outcome, you can stay motivated, focused, and inspired, even in the face of challenges. So take some time each day to visualize your dreams, and watch as your life begins to transform before your very eyes.

23: Hope and Leadership: Inspiring Others to Believe in the Possibilities

Leadership is all about inspiring others to believe in the possibilities. It's about creating a vision for the future and inspiring others to work towards that vision. And at the heart of effective leadership is hope. Leaders who have hope and can inspire hope in others are more likely to be successful in achieving their goals.

In this chapter, we'll explore the connection between hope and leadership, and how leaders can cultivate hope in themselves and others.

Hope is a powerful force that can help people overcome adversity, achieve their goals, and create positive change in their lives. And when it comes to leadership, hope is essential. As a leader, you need to be able to see the possibilities and inspire others to see them too. You need to be able to envision a better future and work towards making that vision a reality.

Leaders who have hope are more likely to be able to inspire others to follow them. They're able to communicate their vision for the future in a way that resonates with others, and they're able to inspire others to believe that change is possible.

But cultivating hope isn't always easy, especially in the face of adversity. As a leader, you may face setbacks and challenges that can make it difficult to maintain hope. So how can you cultivate hope and inspire hope in others?

One of the most important things you can do as a leader is to be authentic and transparent. People are more likely to follow someone who they trust and who they believe is genuine. So be honest about the challenges you're facing, but also be optimistic about the possibilities. Share your vision for the future and explain how you believe you can get there.

Another important aspect of cultivating hope is to celebrate progress, no matter how small. When people see that progress is being made, they're more likely to believe that change is possible. So make sure to acknowledge and celebrate the achievements of your team, no matter how small they may be.

23: HOPE AND LEADERSHIP: INSPIRING OTHERS TO BELIEVE IN THE POSSIBILITIES

In addition to being authentic and celebrating progress, there are other things you can do to cultivate hope in yourself and others. For example, you can focus on the positive aspects of a situation, even when things seem bleak. You can look for opportunities in every challenge and focus on what you can control.

You can also encourage your team to set goals and work towards achieving them. When people have a sense of purpose and direction, they're more likely to feel hopeful about the future.

Ultimately, cultivating hope is about creating a positive and supportive environment where people feel empowered to take action and make positive changes in their lives. As a leader, it's your job to create this environment and inspire others to believe in the possibilities.

But cultivating hope isn't just important for leaders. It's important for everyone. Whether you're a manager, an employee, a parent, or a friend, cultivating hope can help you to achieve your goals and create positive change in your life.

So if you're struggling to maintain hope in the face of adversity, remember that hope is a choice. You can choose to focus on the possibilities and believe in the power of positive change. And if you're a leader, remember that you have the power to inspire hope in others. By being authentic, celebrating progress, and focusing on the positive, you can create a positive and supportive environment where people feel empowered to make positive changes in their lives.

24: Coping with Chronic Illness: Finding Hope and Meaning

Living with a chronic illness can be incredibly challenging. It can affect every aspect of your life, from your physical health to your mental well-being and your relationships. Coping with a chronic illness can be a difficult journey, but it's important to remember that there is always hope.

In this chapter, we'll explore how to cope with a chronic illness and find hope and meaning in life despite the challenges.

– Accepting the Diagnosis

The first step in coping with a chronic illness is to accept the diagnosis. It's natural to feel overwhelmed and scared when you're first diagnosed, but accepting the reality of your situation is an important part of moving forward.

Acceptance doesn't mean giving up hope. It means acknowledging the reality of your situation and learning to live with it. It also means taking an active role in managing your health and making the most of your life.

– Building a Support System

24: COPING WITH CHRONIC ILLNESS: FINDING HOPE AND MEANING

Living with a chronic illness can be isolating, but it's important to remember that you're not alone. Building a support system of family, friends, and healthcare professionals can help you feel less isolated and more empowered.

Joining a support group can also be helpful. Support groups provide a safe space to share your experiences, learn from others, and gain practical advice for coping with your illness.

– Managing Symptoms and Treatment

Managing the symptoms and treatment of a chronic illness can be a daily challenge. It's important to work closely with your healthcare team to develop a treatment plan that works for you.

This may include medication, therapy, lifestyle changes, or a combination of these approaches. It's also important to listen to your body and rest when you need to.

– Finding Meaning and Purpose

Living with a chronic illness can make it difficult to find meaning and purpose in life. But it's important to remember that you still have value and a purpose, even if your life looks different than you expected.

Finding meaning and purpose may involve exploring new hobbies or interests, volunteering, or connecting with others who share similar experiences.

– Fostering Positive Thinking

Positive thinking is an important part of coping with a chronic illness. Focusing on the positive aspects of your life, rather than dwelling on the negative, can help you feel more hopeful and empowered.

This may involve practicing gratitude, focusing on your strengths, and setting realistic goals for yourself.

– Prioritizing Self-Care

Coping with a chronic illness can be physically and emotionally exhausting. Prioritizing self-care is essential for maintaining your health and well-being.

This may involve getting enough sleep, eating a balanced diet, exercising regularly, and practicing stress-reduction techniques such as meditation or deep breathing.

– Embracing Hope

Finally, it's important to embrace hope. Even in the face of a chronic illness, there is always hope for a better tomorrow.

Hope may come in the form of new treatments, supportive relationships, or personal growth and resilience. It's important to hold onto hope and believe that positive change is possible.

Living with a chronic illness is never easy, but finding hope and meaning can help you cope with the challenges and make the most of your life. By accepting your diagnosis, building a support system, managing your symptoms, finding purpose and meaning, fostering positive thinking, prioritizing self-care, and embracing hope, you can live a fulfilling life despite the challenges.

25: Hope and Social Justice: The Role of Empathy and Compassion

In today's world, social justice is a critical issue that affects individuals and communities around the globe. The fight for equality and fairness is ongoing, and it's essential that we all play a role in creating a better, more just society. In this chapter, we'll explore the important role that empathy and compassion play in promoting social justice and fostering hope for a better future.

– Empathy: Understanding Others' Experiences

Empathy is the ability to understand and share the feelings of others. It's an essential skill for creating connections and building relationships, but it's also crucial for promoting social justice.

When we empathize with others, we're better able to understand their experiences and the challenges they face. This understanding can help us develop a deeper sense of compassion and a greater commitment to promoting social justice.

– Compassion: Taking Action to Help Others

25: HOPE AND SOCIAL JUSTICE: THE ROLE OF EMPATHY AND COMPASSION

Compassion is the act of feeling sympathy and concern for others and taking action to help them. It's an important part of creating positive change in the world.

When we feel compassion for others, we're motivated to take action to help them. This could involve volunteering our time, donating money to a cause we care about, or advocating for change in our communities.

– Listening to Marginalized Voices

One of the most critical aspects of promoting social justice is listening to the voices of marginalized groups. Often, those who are most impacted by inequality and injustice are the ones who are least heard.

By listening to and amplifying the voices of marginalized groups, we can gain a better understanding of their experiences and work to create more inclusive and equitable communities.

– Practicing Inclusion and Equity

Inclusion and equity are essential components of social justice. Inclusion means ensuring that everyone feels welcome and valued, regardless of their background or identity. Equity involves creating fair and just systems that provide equal opportunities for all.

We can practice inclusion and equity in our personal and professional lives by creating diverse and inclusive spaces, advocating for equal treatment and opportunities, and challenging discriminatory practices and policies.

– Educating Ourselves and Others

Education is a powerful tool for promoting social justice. By learning about the experiences of marginalized groups and the ways in which systems of oppression operate, we can develop a deeper understanding of the challenges faced by others and work to create change.

We can educate ourselves by reading books and articles written by marginalized authors, attending workshops and trainings, and seeking out conversations with individuals from diverse backgrounds.

– Taking Action

Finally, it's essential to take action to promote social justice.

25: HOPE AND SOCIAL JUSTICE: THE ROLE OF EMPATHY AND COMPASSION

This could involve getting involved in political or community activism, supporting organizations that promote equality and fairness, or using our voices and platforms to advocate for change.

No matter how small or large our actions may seem, every effort counts towards creating a more just and equitable world.

In conclusion, empathy and compassion are critical tools for promoting social justice and fostering hope for a better future. By practicing empathy and compassion, listening to marginalized voices, promoting inclusion and equity, educating ourselves and others, and taking action, we can all play a role in creating a better, more just society. Let's work together to build a future filled with hope and possibility for all.

26: Overcoming Fear: Building Courage through Hope

Fear is a natural emotion that serves as a protective mechanism to keep us safe from danger. However, when fear becomes overwhelming and all-consuming, it can hold us back from living our lives to the fullest. In this chapter, we'll explore the role that hope plays in building courage and overcoming fear.

– Understanding Fear

Fear is a powerful emotion that can manifest in many different ways. It can cause us to avoid certain situations, take unnecessary risks, or become paralyzed with anxiety. In some cases, fear can even become a phobia, which is an intense and irrational fear of a specific object or situation.

It's important to understand that fear is a normal and necessary part of life. However, when fear becomes overwhelming, it can hold us back from pursuing our goals and living the life we want.

– The Relationship between Fear and Hope

Hope is the belief that things can get better and that we

have the power to make positive changes in our lives. When we have hope, we're able to see beyond our current circumstances and envision a brighter future. This perspective can help us build the courage to face our fears and overcome them.

Hope and fear are two sides of the same coin. When we're faced with a challenging situation, fear may be our initial response. However, when we cultivate hope, we can use it to counteract our fear and build the courage to take action.

– Identifying the Source of Fear

One of the first steps in overcoming fear is identifying its source. Sometimes fear is related to a specific event or circumstance, while other times it may be more general or abstract.

By identifying the source of our fear, we can begin to address it directly and develop strategies to overcome it. This could involve seeking support from friends or professionals, practicing relaxation techniques, or gradually exposing ourselves to the source of our fear in a controlled and safe environment.

26: OVERCOMING FEAR: BUILDING COURAGE THROUGH HOPE

– Developing a Growth Mindset

A growth mindset is the belief that our abilities and intelligence can be developed over time through hard work and dedication. This mindset can be a powerful tool in overcoming fear because it allows us to approach challenges with a sense of curiosity and a willingness to learn.

When we have a growth mindset, we're less likely to be held back by fear of failure or making mistakes. Instead, we see setbacks as opportunities for growth and learning.

– Taking Action

Taking action is a crucial step in overcoming fear. This could involve confronting our fears head-on, seeking support from others, or developing a plan to gradually expose ourselves to the source of our fear.

It's important to remember that taking action doesn't necessarily mean completely overcoming our fear right away. It may be a gradual process, and setbacks and challenges are a natural part of that process.

– Cultivating Hope

26: OVERCOMING FEAR: BUILDING COURAGE THROUGH HOPE

Finally, cultivating hope is an essential part of building courage and overcoming fear. When we have hope, we're able to see beyond our current circumstances and envision a brighter future. This perspective can help us build the courage to face our fears and take action towards our goals.

We can cultivate hope by setting realistic goals, visualizing positive outcomes, and surrounding ourselves with supportive and encouraging people.

In conclusion, fear can be a powerful emotion that holds us back from living our lives to the fullest. However, by cultivating hope, identifying the source of our fear, developing a growth mindset, taking action, and surrounding ourselves with support and encouragement, we can build the courage to overcome our fears and achieve our goals. Remember, hope is a powerful tool for building courage and achieving success in the face of adversity.

27: Hope and Empowerment: Taking Control of Your Life

Introduction

Life is full of ups and downs, and at times, it can feel like we have no control over the direction our lives are taking. We can get lost in the chaos of the world around us and become overwhelmed with the challenges that we face. However, no matter what situation we find ourselves in, we always have the power to take control of our lives, to change our outlook and to embrace hope. In this chapter, we will explore the connection between hope and empowerment and the steps we can take to take control of our lives and achieve our wildest dreams.

The Power of Hope

Hope is a powerful emotion that can transform our lives. It is the belief that we can overcome adversity and achieve our goals despite the challenges that we face. Hope helps us to see the possibilities that lie ahead and to focus on the positive outcomes that we can create.

Hope is not just wishful thinking; it is a belief that we can take action to change our lives. When we have hope, we are more likely to take risks, to try new things, and to persevere in the face of challenges. Hope is the fuel that drives us towards our goals, and it gives us the resilience to keep going when things get tough.

Taking Control of Our Lives

Taking control of our lives begins with understanding that we have the power to shape our future. It is easy to get caught up in the negative aspects of our lives, to focus on the things that we cannot control, and to feel powerless in the face of adversity. However, by focusing on the things that we can control and taking action towards our goals, we can create positive change in our lives.

The first step towards taking control of our lives is to identify the areas that we want to change. This could be anything from improving our health and fitness to advancing our careers or building stronger relationships. Once we have identified the areas that we want to focus on, we can begin to set goals and create a plan to achieve them.

Setting Goals

27: HOPE AND EMPOWERMENT: TAKING CONTROL OF YOUR LIFE

Goals are a powerful tool for creating positive change in our lives. They give us something to strive for and provide a roadmap for achieving our dreams. When we set goals, we are more likely to take action towards achieving them, and we are more likely to stay motivated when we face challenges.

When setting goals, it is important to be specific about what we want to achieve. We should also ensure that our goals are realistic and achievable within a reasonable timeframe. Setting too many goals or setting goals that are too ambitious can lead to feelings of overwhelm and discouragement.

Creating a Plan

Once we have set our goals, we need to create a plan to achieve them. This plan should include specific actions that we can take to move towards our goals. For example, if our goal is to improve our health and fitness, our plan could include actions such as joining a gym, hiring a personal trainer, or creating a meal plan.

It is important to be flexible when creating a plan. We may

need to adjust our plan as we go along to account for unexpected obstacles or changes in circumstances. However, having a plan in place gives us a sense of direction and helps us to stay focused on our goals.

Taking Action

Taking action is the most important step in taking control of our lives. It is easy to get stuck in a cycle of planning without taking action, but action is what creates change. We need to be willing to take risks, try new things, and step outside of our comfort zones if we want to achieve our goals.

When taking action, it is important to focus on progress rather than perfection. We will make mistakes, encounter setbacks, and face challenges along the way, but these are all opportunities for growth and learning. By focusing on progress rather than perfection, we can stay motivated and continue moving towards

28: The Role of Humor in Cultivating Hope

Introduction

Hope is a powerful emotion that can help us overcome adversity and achieve our goals. However, life can be challenging, and it can be difficult to maintain a sense of hope when we are faced with difficult situations. In these moments, humor can play a powerful role in cultivating hope and helping us to maintain a positive outlook. In this chapter, we will explore the role of humor in cultivating hope and the ways in which we can use humor to overcome adversity.

The Benefits of Humor

Humor has many benefits for our mental and emotional well-being. It can help to reduce stress, increase resilience, and improve our overall sense of well-being. When we laugh, our bodies release endorphins, which are natural chemicals that promote a sense of happiness and well-being.

Humor can also help us to cope with difficult situations. It can provide a temporary escape from our problems, and it can help us to see things from a different perspective. Humor can also help us to connect with others and build stronger relationships.

Using Humor to Overcome Adversity

When we are faced with difficult situations, it can be challenging to maintain a sense of hope. However, humor can be a powerful tool for overcoming adversity and cultivating hope.

One way to use humor to overcome adversity is to find the funny side of the situation. This can be challenging, but finding humor in difficult situations can help us to maintain a positive outlook and reduce stress. For example, if we are stuck in traffic, we could try to find humor in the situation by listening to a funny podcast or thinking about how we can use the time to catch up on phone calls or listen to an audiobook.

Humor can also help us to connect with others and build stronger relationships. When we share a laugh with others, we create a sense of camaraderie and connection. This can be especially important during difficult times when we may feel isolated or alone.

Humor can also help us to maintain perspective. When we are faced with difficult situations, it can be easy to become overwhelmed and lose sight of the bigger picture. However, humor can help us to step back and see things from a different perspective. This can help us to maintain a sense of hope and optimism, even in the face of adversity.

Finding Humor in Everyday Life

Humor doesn't just have to be reserved for difficult situations. We can also use humor in our everyday lives to cultivate hope and positivity. One way to do this is to surround ourselves with things that make us laugh. This could be anything from funny memes to humorous books or movies.

We can also make a conscious effort to find humor in our daily lives. This could be as simple as telling a joke or sharing a funny story with a friend or colleague. By finding humor in our everyday lives, we can cultivate a sense of joy and positivity that can help us to maintain a sense of hope and optimism.

Using Humor Responsibly

28: THE ROLE OF HUMOR IN CULTIVATING HOPE

While humor can be a powerful tool for cultivating hope and positivity, it is important to use it responsibly. Humor that is hurtful or offensive can have the opposite effect and can actually increase stress and negativity. It is important to be mindful of our audience and to use humor in a way that is appropriate and respectful.

Conclusion

Humor is a powerful tool for cultivating hope and overcoming adversity. It can help us to maintain a positive outlook, reduce stress, and improve our overall sense of well-being. By finding humor in difficult situations and using humor responsibly in our daily lives, we can cultivate a sense of hope and optimism that can help us to achieve our goals and overcome life's greatest challenges.

29: Hope and Purpose: Finding Meaning in Life's Challenges

Introduction

Life is full of challenges and difficulties that can leave us feeling lost and without purpose. However, hope can provide us with the motivation and inspiration we need to overcome these challenges and find meaning in our lives. In this chapter, we will explore the relationship between hope and purpose, and how we can use hope to find meaning in life's challenges.

The Importance of Purpose

Having a sense of purpose is essential for our mental and emotional well-being. It gives us a reason to get up in the morning and motivates us to pursue our goals and aspirations. Purpose also provides us with a sense of meaning and fulfillment, which can improve our overall sense of well-being.

However, finding our purpose can be challenging, especially when we are faced with difficult situations. It can be easy to lose sight of our goals and aspirations when we are struggling to overcome adversity.

The Role of Hope in Finding Purpose

Hope can play a powerful role in helping us to find purpose in life's challenges. When we have hope, we are able to maintain a positive outlook and see the potential for growth and development, even in the face of adversity.

Hope can also provide us with the motivation and inspiration we need to pursue our goals and find meaning in our lives. When we have hope, we are more likely to take risks and pursue opportunities that can help us to achieve our aspirations.

In addition, hope can help us to maintain perspective when we are faced with difficult situations. It can remind us that our current challenges are only temporary and that we have the ability to overcome them and find meaning in the process.

Finding Purpose in Adversity

One of the most powerful ways that we can find purpose in life's challenges is by using them as opportunities for growth and development. Adversity can be a powerful teacher, and it can help us to develop new skills, strengths, and perspectives.

When we approach adversity with hope, we are able to see the potential for growth and development, even in the most difficult situations. This can help us to find purpose in the process of overcoming our challenges and achieving our goals.

Another way to find purpose in adversity is by helping others who are facing similar challenges. By sharing our experiences and offering support and encouragement, we can help others to find hope and purpose in their own lives.

Finding Purpose in Everyday Life

Purpose doesn't have to be reserved for major life events or challenges. We can find purpose in our everyday lives by focusing on the things that bring us joy and fulfillment.

This could be anything from pursuing a hobby or passion to volunteering for a cause that we are passionate about. By focusing on the things that bring us joy and fulfillment, we can find meaning and purpose in our daily lives.

Conclusion

Hope and purpose are intimately linked, and cultivating hope can help us to find meaning in life's challenges. By maintaining a positive outlook, taking risks, and seeing adversity as an opportunity for growth and development, we can find purpose in the process of overcoming our challenges and achieving our goals. Whether we are facing major life events or simply looking for purpose in our daily lives, hope can provide us with the motivation and inspiration we need to find meaning and fulfillment.

30: The Power of Self-Talk: Harnessing Positive Language for Hope

Introduction

Our internal dialogue, or self-talk, can have a significant impact on our mental and emotional well-being. Negative self-talk can contribute to feelings of hopelessness and despair, while positive self-talk can inspire hope and resilience. In this chapter, we will explore the power of self-talk and how we can use positive language to cultivate hope and achieve our goals.

Understanding Self-Talk

Self-talk refers to the internal dialogue that we have with ourselves throughout the day. It can be both positive and negative, and it often goes unnoticed. Negative self-talk can be damaging to our self-esteem and mental health, while positive self-talk can help us to build resilience and cultivate hope.

Negative self-talk often takes the form of self-criticism, self-doubt, and negative self-evaluation. It can include thoughts like, "I'm not good enough," "I'll never succeed," or "I always mess things up." These thoughts can be automatic and difficult to control, but they can contribute to feelings of hopelessness and despair.

Positive self-talk, on the other hand, involves using encouraging and supportive language to inspire hope and motivation. It can include thoughts like, "I am capable of overcoming challenges," "I am making progress towards my goals," or "I am deserving of success." By consciously using positive self-talk, we can reframe our thoughts and cultivate a sense of hope and optimism.

The Benefits of Positive Self-Talk

Positive self-talk can have a range of benefits for our mental and emotional well-being. Some of these benefits include:

– Increased self-esteem: When we use positive self-talk, we are reinforcing positive beliefs about ourselves and our abilities. This can help to increase our self-esteem and self-worth.

– Greater resilience: Positive self-talk can help us to bounce

back from setbacks and challenges. By maintaining a positive outlook, we can build resilience and cultivate hope, even
in difficult situations.

— Improved motivation: Positive self-talk can provide us
with the motivation and inspiration we need to pursue our
goals and aspirations. By focusing on our strengths and
abilities, we can stay motivated and achieve our dreams.

— Reduced stress and anxiety: Negative self-talk can contribute to feelings of stress and anxiety, while positive self-
talk can help to reduce these feelings. By reframing our
thoughts and focusing on the positive, we can reduce the
impact of stress and anxiety on our lives.

Tips for Using Positive Self-Talk

— Pay attention to your thoughts: The first step in harnessing the power of positive self-talk is to become aware of
your thoughts. Take note of any negative self-talk that you
engage in throughout the day and make an effort to reframe
those thoughts in a positive way.

— Use encouraging language: When engaging in positive

self-talk, use language that is encouraging and supportive. Use words like "I can," "I will," and "I am capable of" to reinforce positive beliefs about yourself.

– Focus on your strengths: When using positive self-talk, focus on your strengths and abilities. Remind yourself of the things that you are good at and the progress that you have made towards your goals.

– Practice self-compassion: When engaging in positive self-talk, it is important to be compassionate towards yourself. Recognize that you are human and that it is okay to make mistakes. Treat yourself with kindness and understanding, and focus on the progress that you are making rather than perfection.

Conclusion

Positive self-talk can be a powerful tool for cultivating hope and achieving our goals. By becoming aware of our thoughts and using encouraging and supportive language, we can reframe our internal dialogue and cultivate a sense of hope and optimism. With practice and persistence, positive self-talk can help us to build resilience, increase our self-esteem, and achieve our wildest dreams. Remember that using positive self-talk is not about denying the challenges or difficulties that we may face, but rather about approaching them with a positive mindset and a belief in our ability to overcome them.

As we continue to practice positive self-talk, we may find that it becomes easier to maintain a hopeful outlook even in the face of adversity. We may also find that our relationships with others improve, as we are more positive and supportive towards those around us. Ultimately, the power of positive self-talk lies in its ability to shape our perception of ourselves and the world around us. By choosing to focus on the positive and using encouraging language, we can cultivate a sense of hope and resilience that will serve us well throughout our lives.

So, if you find yourself engaging in negative self-talk, remember that you have the power to change your thoughts and your outlook. Start by becoming aware of your thoughts and making a conscious effort to reframe them in a positive way. Use encouraging and supportive language, focus on your strengths and abilities, and practice self-compassion.

30: THE POWER OF SELF-TALK: HARNESSING POSIT-IVE LANGUAGE FOR HOPE

With time and practice, positive self-talk can become a habit that helps you to approach life's challenges with hope and optimism.

31: Overcoming Adversity: Lessons from Those Who Have Triumphed

Adversity is an inevitable part of life, and we will all face challenges and setbacks at some point. Whether it's dealing with illness, loss, financial struggles, or other difficult circumstances, it's easy to feel overwhelmed and hopeless when things don't go as planned. However, it's important to remember that adversity can also be an opportunity for growth and learning.

Throughout history, there have been countless examples of people who have faced incredible challenges and emerged stronger and more resilient as a result. These individuals have shown us that it's possible to overcome even the most difficult circumstances and achieve great things.

One such example is Oprah Winfrey, who was born into poverty in Mississippi and faced numerous obstacles throughout her life, including childhood abuse, discrimination, and struggles with her weight. Despite these challenges, she was able to build a successful career as a media mogul, philanthropist, and advocate for social justice. In her own words, "I believe that one of life's greatest lessons is that no matter how hard the road, keep moving forward."

Another example is Nick Vujicic, who was born without arms or legs and faced bullying and discrimination growing up. Despite these challenges, he has become a motivational speaker and author, inspiring millions of people around the world with his message of hope and resilience. As he says, "If I fail, I try again, and again, and again. If you fail, are you going to try again?"

These examples show us that adversity doesn't have to define us or limit our potential. In fact, it can be a catalyst for growth and transformation if we choose to approach it with a positive mindset and a sense of hope.

So how can we overcome adversity and emerge stronger and more resilient? Here are some lessons we can learn from those who have triumphed over adversity:

– Embrace your challenges: Rather than avoiding or denying your challenges, embrace them as opportunities for growth and learning. As Oprah Winfrey has said, "Challenges are gifts that force us to search for a new center of gravity. Don't fight them. Just find a different way to stand."

— Find meaning in your struggles: Look for ways to find meaning and purpose in your struggles. For example, Nick Vujicic has used his own experiences to inspire others and help them overcome their own challenges.

— Develop a positive mindset: Choose to focus on the positive and cultivate a sense of hope and optimism, even in the face of adversity. As Nick Vujicic says, "The greatest disability is not having limbs, the greatest disability is having a negative mindset."

— Seek support: Don't be afraid to ask for help and support from others, whether it's friends, family, or professionals. As Oprah Winfrey has said, "Surround yourself with only people who are going to lift you higher."

— Take action: Rather than feeling helpless or overwhelmed, take action to address your challenges and work towards your goals. As Nick Vujicic says, "I will try one hundred times to get up, and if I fail one hundred times. If I fail and I give up, will I ever get up? No!"

31: OVERCOMING ADVERSITY: LESSONS FROM THOSE WHO HAVE TRIUMPHED

By embracing these lessons and cultivating a sense of hope and resilience, we can overcome even the most difficult challenges and emerge stronger and more empowered than ever before. Remember, as Oprah Winfrey has said, "The greatest discovery of all time is that a person can change his future by merely changing his attitude."

Another great example of overcoming adversity is the story of Nick Vujicic, an Australian motivational speaker born without arms or legs. Despite his physical challenges, Vujicic has accomplished incredible feats and inspired millions around the world.

From a young age, Vujicic struggled with depression and suicidal thoughts due to his physical limitations. However, with the help of his faith, supportive family, and a determination to live a full life, he overcame his struggles and began to spread hope and positivity to others.

Vujicic's message is one of resilience and perseverance in the face of adversity. He reminds us that our struggles do not define us and that we have the power to choose our own attitudes and reactions to difficult situations.

31: OVERCOMING ADVERSITY: LESSONS FROM THOSE WHO HAVE TRIUMPHED

Another inspiring figure is Malala Yousafzai, a Pakistani activist for female education and the youngest Nobel Prize laureate. At just 15 years old, Malala was shot in the head by a Taliban gunman for her advocacy work. Miraculously, she survived and continued her work, becoming a global symbol of the fight for girls' education.

Malala's story is a testament to the power of hope and the importance of standing up for what you believe in. Despite facing intense opposition and danger, she remained committed to her mission and refused to be silenced.

These examples demonstrate that while adversity can be challenging and painful, it can also be an opportunity for growth, learning, and transformation. When we face difficulties with hope, resilience, and a determination to overcome, we can emerge stronger and more resilient than before.

32: The Benefits of Hope: Improved Well-Being and Quality of Life

Hope is a powerful force that can have profound effects on our well-being and quality of life. Research has shown that individuals who possess a high level of hope tend to experience better physical health, psychological well-being, and social connectedness.

One of the main benefits of hope is improved mental health. Studies have found that hope is associated with lower levels of depression, anxiety, and stress. When we have hope, we are better able to cope with the challenges and stresses of life, and are less likely to experience negative emotions.

In addition to its positive impact on mental health, hope has also been linked to better physical health outcomes. Individuals with higher levels of hope tend to have lower levels of inflammation, lower rates of chronic disease, and a faster recovery from illness or injury.

Furthermore, hope can improve our social connections and relationships. People who are hopeful are more likely to engage in positive social interactions, build supportive relationships, and feel a greater sense of belonging.

One study found that hope was a significant predictor of life satisfaction, even when controlling for factors such as income, education, and age. This suggests that hope may play a vital role in our overall sense of well-being and happiness.

In addition to the positive effects on individuals, hope can also have a ripple effect on communities and society as a whole. When we have hope, we are more likely to engage in positive behaviors and contribute to our communities in meaningful ways.

For example, individuals with higher levels of hope tend to be more motivated, persistent, and goal-oriented. They are more likely to take actions that lead to positive outcomes, such as pursuing education or training, seeking out opportunities for personal growth, or volunteering their time and resources to help others.

Moreover, hope can inspire and empower others. When we see others overcoming challenges and achieving their goals, it can inspire us to do the same. This creates a positive feedback loop, where hope begets hope, and individuals and communities are uplifted and transformed.

In conclusion, the benefits of hope are manifold and far-reaching. Whether we are facing difficult circumstances, pursuing personal goals, or seeking to make a positive impact on the world around us, hope is a powerful tool that can help us achieve our full potential and experience greater well-being and fulfillment.

33: The Role of Resilience in Hope: Building Strength for the Journey

Resilience is the ability to bounce back from adversity, to recover from setbacks and challenges, and to adapt and grow in the face of difficult circumstances. It is an essential component of hope, enabling us to face the inevitable challenges of life with strength and courage.

Resilience is not a fixed trait that some people have and others do not. Rather, it is a set of skills and attitudes that can be developed and strengthened over time. By building resilience, we can increase our capacity for hope, and become more resilient in the face of adversity.

One of the key factors that contributes to resilience is optimism. Optimism is the belief that good things can happen, and that we have the power to make positive changes in our lives. When we are optimistic, we are more likely to view setbacks and challenges as temporary and surmountable, rather than insurmountable obstacles.

Another important factor in building resilience is social support. Having a network of supportive friends, family, and community members can provide us with the emotional support, encouragement, and practical assistance we need to navigate difficult times.

Resilience is also closely linked to self-care. Taking care of ourselves physically, emotionally, and mentally can help us to cope with stress and maintain a positive outlook, even in the face of adversity. This includes getting enough sleep, eating well, exercising regularly, and engaging in activities that bring us joy and fulfillment.

Additionally, resilience involves developing coping strategies that help us to manage stress and regulate our emotions. This may involve techniques such as mindfulness, meditation, deep breathing, or cognitive-behavioral therapy.

Ultimately, building resilience is a lifelong process that requires commitment, effort, and persistence. However, the rewards of cultivating resilience are significant. By strengthening our capacity for hope and resilience, we can face life's challenges with greater confidence, and emerge from difficult times stronger, wiser, and more compassionate.

33: THE ROLE OF RESILIENCE IN HOPE: BUILDING STRENGTH FOR THE JOURNEY

Resilience also enables us to pursue our goals and aspirations, even in the face of obstacles and setbacks. It allows us to stay focused on what is important, and to remain committed to our values and beliefs, even in the midst of adversity.

In conclusion, resilience is an essential component of hope, enabling us to build strength and resilience for the journey of life. By cultivating resilience through optimism, social support, self-care, and coping strategies, we can become more resilient, and more hopeful, in the face of life's greatest challenges.

34: Hope and Success: Achieving Your Wildest Dreams

One of the most powerful benefits of cultivating hope is the ability to achieve our wildest dreams. Hope gives us the motivation and determination to set goals and work towards them, even when obstacles arise. It helps us maintain a positive outlook on life, and provides us with the resilience we need to overcome setbacks and failures.

Success can mean different things to different people, and it's important to define what success means to you. It could mean achieving financial stability, reaching a certain career goal, starting a family, or even just being content with where you are in life. Whatever your definition of success may be, hope can help you achieve it.

Here are some ways in which hope can help you achieve success:

– Setting Realistic Goals: Hope helps us set realistic goals for ourselves. It encourages us to dream big, but also to break down those big dreams into smaller, more achievable goals. By setting realistic goals, we can measure our progress and stay motivated.

34: HOPE AND SUCCESS: ACHIEVING YOUR WILDEST DREAMS

– Taking Action: Hope gives us the motivation we need to take action towards our goals. Instead of just wishing for success, we take steps towards achieving it. We believe that our actions will make a difference, and that we have the power to change our circumstances.

– Persevering Through Obstacles: No journey towards success is without obstacles. Hope gives us the resilience we need to push through those obstacles and keep moving forward. We don't give up at the first sign of failure, but instead see failure as an opportunity to learn and grow.

– Overcoming Fear: Fear is one of the biggest obstacles to success. We may fear failure, or even fear success itself. Hope helps us overcome that fear by providing us with the courage to take risks and step outside of our comfort zones.

– Maintaining a Positive Outlook: Finally, hope helps us maintain a positive outlook on life, even when things get tough. By focusing on the good, we can keep ourselves motivated and hopeful, even when faced with setbacks and failures.

Of course, cultivating hope alone is not enough to guarantee success. Success also requires hard work, dedication, and a willingness to learn and grow. But by cultivating hope, we give ourselves the best possible chance of achieving our wildest dreams.

Here are some tips for cultivating hope and achieving success:

– Visualize Your Goals: Take some time to visualize your goals and what it will feel like to achieve them. This helps to make your goals more real and tangible, and provides you with motivation to work towards them.

– Break Your Goals Down: Break your big goals down into smaller, more achievable goals. This helps you measure your progress and stay motivated.

– Take Action: Don't just wish for success – take action towards it. Start with small steps, and work your way up. Every action you take brings you closer to your goals.

– Don't Be Afraid to Fail: Failure is a natural part of the journey towards success. Instead of seeing failure as a setback, see it as an opportunity to learn and grow.

34: HOPE AND SUCCESS: ACHIEVING YOUR WILDEST DREAMS

– Surround Yourself with Positive People: Surround your-self with people who support and encourage you. Having a support system can make all the difference when it comes to achieving success.

– Practice Self-Care: Taking care of yourself is essential for cultivating hope and achieving success. Make sure to get enough sleep, eat a healthy diet, and take time to relax and recharge.

Another important aspect of achieving success through hope is to remain flexible and adaptable. No plan or strategy is foolproof, and there may be setbacks and unfore-seen obstacles that require a change in approach. Rather than becoming discouraged or giving up when faced with these challenges, those with hope will adapt and modify their plans as needed to continue working towards their goals.

Additionally, it is important to remember that success is not always immediate or linear. There may be setbacks and fail-ures along the way, but those with hope understand that these are just temporary roadblocks and keep pushing for-ward. They also celebrate their small victories along the way, recognizing that each step towards their goal is progress and reason to be hopeful for the future.

Finally, those who achieve success through hope understand the importance of taking action. It is not enough to simply hope for something to happen, but rather to take consistent and deliberate action towards achieving it. This may require stepping outside of one's comfort zone and taking risks, but those with hope are willing to do so in pursuit of their goals.

In conclusion, hope plays a crucial role in achieving success in all areas of life. By cultivating a positive outlook, setting goals, remaining flexible and adaptable, celebrating small victories, and taking consistent action, anyone can harness the power of hope to achieve their wildest dreams. Remember, no matter what challenges or setbacks may arise, there is always reason to remain hopeful for the future.

35: Hope and Legacy: Leaving a Positive Impact on the World

Introduction:

What kind of impact do we want to leave on the world? This question has been asked by many people throughout history. Some people want to be remembered for their accomplishments, while others want to be remembered for their kindness or their impact on the world around them. Leaving a positive legacy is something that many of us strive for, but how do we go about doing that? In this chapter, we'll explore the role of hope in leaving a positive impact on the world.

The Importance of Legacy:

Leaving a positive legacy is important for a number of reasons. For one, it can give us a sense of purpose and meaning in our lives. When we know that we are making a positive impact on the world, we feel more fulfilled and happier. Additionally, leaving a positive legacy can inspire others to do the same. When we see someone making a positive impact on the world, it can motivate us to do the same.

35: HOPE AND LEGACY: LEAVING A POSITIVE IMPACT ON THE WORLD

The Role of Hope:

Hope plays a significant role in leaving a positive legacy. When we have hope for the future, we are more likely to take action to create the world that we want to see. Hope can motivate us to work towards our goals and to make a positive impact on the world around us. When we have hope, we believe that change is possible, and we are more likely to take steps to make that change happen.

Hope also helps us to persevere in the face of challenges. When we encounter obstacles or setbacks, hope can help us to keep going. We believe that there is a way to overcome these challenges and to continue making progress towards our goals.

Leaving a Positive Legacy:

So, how do we go about leaving a positive legacy? There are a number of ways that we can make a positive impact on the world around us. Here are just a few:

– Volunteer: Volunteering is a great way to make a positive impact on your community. There are many organizations and causes that could use your help, whether it's a local food bank, animal shelter, or community center. By giving your time and energy to these organizations, you can make a real difference in the lives of others.

– Be Kind: Sometimes the smallest acts of kindness can have a big impact on others. Whether it's holding the door open for someone or giving someone a compliment, these small acts can make a big difference in someone's day.

– Advocate for Change: If there's a cause that you're passionate about, speak up! Advocating for change can take many forms, from signing petitions to attending rallies to contacting your elected officials. By speaking out about the issues that matter to you, you can help to create change in the world.

– Lead by Example: One of the best ways to make a positive impact on the world is to lead by example. When we live our lives with integrity, kindness, and compassion, we inspire others to do the same. By being the change that we want to see in the world, we can leave a positive legacy that will inspire others for years to come.

35: HOPE AND LEGACY: LEAVING A POSITIVE IMPACT ON THE WORLD

Conclusion:

Leaving a positive legacy is something that many of us aspire to do. By making a positive impact on the world around us, we can create a better future for ourselves and for future generations. Hope plays a critical role in leaving a positive legacy, by motivating us to take action and by helping us to persevere in the face of challenges. Whether we choose to volunteer, be kind, advocate for change, or lead by example, we can all make a difference in the world. So, let's embrace hope and work towards leaving a positive legacy that will inspire others for generations to come.

36: Living a Hopeful Life: Embracing the Power of Hope Every Day

Introduction

Hope is not just an emotion, it is a way of life. Living a hopeful life means embracing the power of hope every day, in every aspect of our lives. It means seeing the potential in ourselves and others, even in the midst of challenges and setbacks. It means being proactive in pursuing our dreams and goals, and believing in our ability to overcome obstacles along the way.

In this chapter, we will explore the key principles and strategies for living a hopeful life, from cultivating a positive mindset and nurturing meaningful relationships to practicing gratitude and embracing change. We will also look at the practical steps you can take to bring more hope into your daily routine, and how to maintain a hopeful perspective even in the face of adversity.

Cultivating a Positive Mindset

The first step in living a hopeful life is cultivating a positive mindset. This means learning to focus on the positive aspects of your life, rather than dwelling on the negative. It means developing a sense of optimism, even when things don't go as planned.

One way to cultivate a positive mindset is to practice mindfulness. Mindfulness is the practice of being fully present in the moment, without judgment or distraction. By focusing on the present moment, you can let go of worries about the past or fears about the future. You can also learn to appreciate the simple pleasures in life, such as the taste of your morning coffee or the sound of birds chirping outside your window.

Another way to cultivate a positive mindset is to practice self-compassion. Self-compassion is the practice of treating yourself with the same kindness and understanding that you would offer to a good friend. This means acknowledging your own flaws and imperfections, without being overly critical or judgmental. By practicing self-compassion, you can learn to be more forgiving of yourself and others, and to let go of negative self-talk and self-doubt.

Nurturing Meaningful Relationships

Another key component of living a hopeful life is nurturing meaningful relationships. This means surrounding yourself with positive, supportive people who share your values and beliefs. It also means investing time and energy into building and maintaining these relationships, whether it's through regular phone calls, social outings, or just checking in on each other from time to time.

One way to nurture meaningful relationships is to practice active listening. Active listening means giving your full attention to the person you're talking to, without interrupting or judging them. It also means asking questions and offering supportive feedback, rather than just waiting for your turn to speak. By practicing active listening, you can deepen your connections with others and build stronger, more meaningful relationships.

Another way to nurture meaningful relationships is to practice forgiveness. Forgiveness means letting go of grudges and resentments, and choosing to focus on the positive aspects of your relationships instead. It also means being willing to apologize and make amends when you've hurt someone else, and to forgive others when they've hurt you.

By practicing forgiveness, you can create a more positive and supportive social network, and strengthen your connections with those around you.

Practicing Gratitude

Gratitude is another key component of living a hopeful life. Gratitude means acknowledging and appreciating the good things in your life, no matter how small or seemingly insignificant. It also means focusing on what you have, rather than what you don't have.

One way to practice gratitude is to keep a gratitude journal. A gratitude journal is a simple notebook where you can write down things you're grateful for each day, whether it's a sunny day, a delicious meal, or a kind gesture from a friend. By focusing on the positive aspects of your life, you can cultivate a sense of gratitude and contentment, and become more resilient in the face of challenges and setbacks.

It's important to recognize that hope is not a one-time event or a fleeting feeling. Rather, it's a way of life that requires continuous cultivation and practice. Living a hopeful life means actively embracing the power of hope every day, even in the face of adversity.

One way to do this is by intentionally focusing on the positive aspects of life, no matter how small they may be. This can involve keeping a gratitude journal, where you write down three things you're grateful for each day, or simply taking a few moments each morning to appreciate the beauty of nature or the warmth of the sun on your face.

Another way to cultivate hope is by setting realistic and achievable goals for yourself. These goals can be related to any area of your life, from your career and finances to your personal relationships and hobbies. By working towards something that's meaningful and fulfilling to you, you can feel a sense of purpose and direction that can help you stay hopeful even in difficult times.

It's also important to surround yourself with positive influences and support systems. This can include friends and family members who uplift and encourage you, as well as professional resources such as therapists or support groups. When you have a community of people who believe in you and your ability to overcome challenges, it can be easier to maintain a sense of hope and resilience.

36: LIVING A HOPEFUL LIFE: EMBRACING THE POWER OF HOPE EVERY DAY

Finally, it's important to remember that hope is not a guarantee of a perfect life without challenges or setbacks. Rather, it's a mindset and a tool that can help you navigate those challenges with greater ease and resilience. By embracing the power of hope and making it a daily practice, you can live a more fulfilling and meaningful life, even in the face of adversity.

Thank You

As we reach the end of this book, I want to say thanks for reading this book.

I want to get this information out to as many people as possible. If you found this book helpful, I would greatly appreciate you leaving me a review. This helps others find the book as well.

Disclaimer

This document is geared towards providing exact and reliable information in regards to the topic and issue covered. The publication is sold on the idea that the publisher is not required to render an accounting, officially permitted, or otherwise, qualified services. If advice is necessary, legal, financial, medical or professional, a practiced individual in the profession should be ordered.

This information is not presented by a financial or medical practitioner and is for entertainment, educational and informational purposes only. The content is not intended as a substitute for professional medical advice, diagnosis, or treatment. Always seek the advice of your physician or other qualified health care provider with any questions you may have regarding a medical condition. Never disregard professional medical advice or delay in seeking it because of something you have read.

The information provided herein is stated to be truthful and consistent, in that any liability, in terms of inattention or otherwise, by any usage or abuse of any policies, processes, or directions contained within is the solitary and utter responsibility of the recipient reader. Under no circumstances

DISCLAIMER

will any legal responsibility or blame be held against the publisher for any reparation, damages, or monetary loss due to the information herein, either directly or indirectly.